Sex Secrets For Men

33 Sex Secret All Men Wish You Knew but Will Never Tell You

Melissa Christopher

ISBN-13: 9798687582940

Little Background Story About Me

My name is Melissa who lives in a small town called Wimberley in Texas, U.S.A. I am a writer though not necessarily a relationship advice writer but I was compelled to write this short but informative and relationship saving book for ladies after learning different things from my man that I never knew.

Earlier when I started dating my man, I made a lot of mistake with him because I didn't know what and what he wanted in bed so I typically assumed and did what I thought was good for him until one day all hell was let loose.

I found out that I had been doing everything all wrong and he wanted something else. It took extra work from me to save my relationship and I decided to put everything I found along the way into a book that can also help other ladies like me either still dating or are married.

I look forward to you enjoying this book and also discovering new things you didn't know yet or confirming some things you already know and do in your relationship.

Thank you for reading this great book till the end.

TABLE OF CONTENT

I really can't thank you enough for making the decision to read this book specially written for "women that care". I appreciate that you chose to get this book that will reveal to you hottest sex secret men wish you knew but will never tell you among other thousands of books on similar topic.

I really appreciate once again. Talking about care, Women that care about being the best for their man, knowing what he wants in bed and giving it to him.

Have you ever been in a situation you wished your partner knew what you wanted and gave it to you without you having to tell him?

If you have ever been in this situation, I'm sure you can easily relate to why he will not be the one to tell you some of the tips I will reveal in this book.

All the tips that are discussed in the book are not based on guess work. These tips were compiled from feedbacks from real men pouring out there mind and revealing some sex secret they wish women know.

There are some things that men wish women knew about sex. Some of them I'm sure most women are at least a little aware of and others maybe not.

It is important to know your partner, know what he wants and explore with him. Not only is this fun and exciting but it allows deeper connections to be established in the relationship.

Here Is List of 33 Sex Secrets Men Wish Women Knew About Them And Sex.

Sex Secret #1 - Men Aren't Insatiable

There is no disputing the fact that men love sex but that doesn't mean they are insatiable and the urge for constant sex should be resisted because doing that will only ruin the intimacy in your relationship.

Women often think that men need sex constantly and are generally insatiable. Some look at this as something that has to be dealt with when instead it should be something to be enjoyed. A relationship where both partner don't feel like the other is insatiable blossoms more than when it is the other way round.

Sex Secret #2 - For Men, Sex Is A Celebration Of Their Connection To Their Partner

Men treat sex as a celebration and as something fun to do with their partner. With this in mind, many wish that women would approach sex with a more liberal mentality.

There are enough things in life that are difficult and complicated, requiring time and focus, sex should be enjoyed and celebrated for the pleasure and joy it allows. So you too also should see sex with your partner as a celebration and something that should be fun at all times.

The connection your man feels with you through sex is very important to sustaining your relationship so you should not overlook it as one of those things that are just by the way.

Sex Secret #3 - Sex Shouldn't Be A Gift That Is Given As A Reward Or On Special Occasions

Women shouldn't treat sex as something they give to men as a gift. Some of these habits compound the hesitancy that many men have when it comes to forming intimate bonds and each of these complications can be remedied with simple communications.

Once you start thinking of sex with your partner as a gift to him and he knows, you have started undoing your relationship with him. This doesn't mean you cant give him a mind-blowing sex when he does something you appreciate, but making it feel like; here is your gift for this, you are already spelling the dome of your relationship.

Make sex part of your relationship irrespective of him doing something for you or not, Sex is an integral part of any happy relationship.

Sex Secret #4 - Make Time For Sex A Priority

Men do love sex, but so do women. Men treat this act as a celebration of their relationship and of their time with their partner. Life today is so demanding that it sometimes difficult to find time for anything as fun and pleasing as sex.

Schedules don't allow free time or for meaningful alone time. Perhaps there are children involved and other complicated work requirements that weigh heavily on both of you. All of these things can limit the time that is available for both of you to spend time together and enjoying one another's company.

Because of this, it is important for a woman to make time to have sex with her partner. Men know what is going on around the house or with work and child schedules but it is important that sex with him be a priority as well.

Sex Secret #5 - Show Them That The Relationship, And Sex With Him Is Important

When a woman constantly tell their man who is asking for sex that they just don't have time right now and maybe after this list of things is done it devalues the man and makes him feel like he is less important.

Sometimes, you can be very busy and not really have the space to make out time for sex when he ask but you can pay him back in kind by coming to him when you are done, that is if what you are doing is really important, also be careful the way you tell him off by making sure he understands.

You need to be able to make him feel like you don't see his need to be less important to you so that he doesn't feel less important and you should always endeavor to make it up to him when you complete whatever you are doing.

Sex allows a woman to show a man that she wants him and that she loves him. By constantly refusing sex or valuing anything else over having time to have pleasure with her partner a woman can damage even the strongest relationship.

Sex is an integral part of any happy relationship, I'm sure you know that already so its very important that you constantly bring you A game to the bedroom. Your man wants to feel loved. One of the easy ways to show him that you love him and that you want him around you and inside you is through sex.

The more you let him enjoy you in the bedroom or the more you show him you want him, the more he gets committed to you.

Sex in itself allows a man to form a deeper and stronger connection with his partner. It is vitally important to make time or even just go with it when the time feels right if the relationship is important.

Men don't necessarily want sex only for the fun of it, they know that they more intimate time they spend with you, they stronger and deeper the bond they have with you.

Aside sex being fun for men, Sex serves as a way to build a strong and deep bond with women and they men wants you to know that. They want you to appreciate that when they ask for sex, it also because they want a stronger and deeper bond with you.

It's almost impossible for a man to claim he loves you but doesn't want to have sex with you. Every man in love wants to have sex with their lover that's why its is called Love Making and they more he enjoys spending intimate time with you, they stronger and deeper the bond is.

Sex Secret #8 - Just Go with it!

Many men wish that women would approach sex more casually and with a bit more abandon. When the time is right, both parties just need to go with the flow and enjoy each other's company.

Sometimes sex needs to be spontaneous, needs to be unexpected because when its like that, you tend to enjoy it more. This explains why some men love to have sex at unusual places outside the bedroom or the house.

Sometimes your man can ask for sex at a very unusual place, that doesn't mean he is a pervert or a jerk, if its okay by you, you should give it a try and see how much fun you both will have.

If you have not tried sex at the backseat, in the swimming pool, at a party, you should give it a try sometimes, you will definitely enjoy it.

If both partners are aware of one another and focused on the pleasure of their partner then there is no reason to be shy or apprehensive about sex.

Men love women who can express themselves in the bedroom. They like an active woman who knows what she wants, knows how to ask for it and knows how to get it.

Sex tends to be boring to guys when their women don't express herself during because she's shy. If you are naturally the shy type or someone that has been made to believe that women who are outspoken or take charge during sex are whores, you need to get that out of your mind and get into the act more. You need to be outspoken in the bedroom, don't be afraid to take charge, speak out in bed.

Ladies who do not alter a word during sex are believed to be boring to men. You need to be talk during sex, you need to express yourself in the best way possible. Say whatever comes to your mind, don't be afraid that he will think you are not making sense.

Sometimes, during sex with my man, I say things I don't know the meaning because something I just want to explode from within when my man is hitting it right. This improves their confidence both during and after sex and can increase their arousal as well. Learn to communicate during sex with your partner.

Sex Secret #11 - Tell Them When They Hit The Right Spot

Aside from telling him what you want in bed, or expressing yourself, you also need to help him know when he is hitting it right.

Having a woman tell them that they are hitting the right spot or that what they are doing feels good, lets the man know that he is getting it right and should continue.

If you have had the awkward experience when you notice that you man looks a bit confused when he is trying something with you in bed and he expect some sort of response and he doesn't get any, you will understand the important of telling him when he is hitting the right spot.

Since everyone is different and is turned on by different things and sensitive to different positions, it is useful for the man to know what position or movement is pleasurable for you without having to guess.

Help him be better as satisfying you in bed so that he relishes spending time with you in bed without looking confused or not knowing what to do to please you. Men sometimes feel lazy in bed and are not ready to go all the way to get you to that point you are shouting his names but when he knows exactly what to do, he goes for the kill straight while still confident that he did it right.

Sex Secret #12 - It's Not A Fear Of Intimacy

While men wish that women approached sex with less hesitation they also resist the bonds that can be formed by this intimate act.

Women often think that men are outright afraid of intimacy and commitment when the hesitancy that can be seen is actually the man withdrawing because he can tell how much he likes having his partner there.

Men are often desperate for intimacy and connection. Because of this, when it is offered by a woman and readily available they sometimes retreat simply because they want it so much.

Sex Secret #13 - Let Him Have His Space After Sex If He Needs It

Yeah, sometimes I get pissed off when my man doesn't want anything to do with me just immediately after having sex with me but men are men and sometimes they just want to be left alone not necessarily because they want to hurt you or show you they don't want you around.

Women need to acknowledge this behavior and instead of being hurt when he turns away after sex, understand that he just needs a few minutes to himself.

By acknowledging this, the woman can reassure him that these feelings are alright and that intimacy and connection are safe and won't be withdrawn.

If a woman is having sex because she feels like she should but she doesn't particularly want to, it will be clear to her partner and will damage the relationship. Sex is part of how a woman makes a man feel loved and needed.

If it is approached as a chore then the man and the relationship are being devalued and disrespected. Behaviors like that can also go a long way to make a man question the solidity of the relationship and of the bonds and intimacy that exists within the relationship.

If these bonds are questioned then he may withdraw further from the relationship and seek loving and caring attention elsewhere.

Sex Secret #15 - Women Need To Be Present And Active In Their Sexual Relationship

Women need to be present and active in their sexual relationship with men. This is the only solid way that they can reassure their partner that their connection is true and reliable. This trust is what allows men to get past their fear of intimacy and allow the bonds and connections that can grow between an intimate couple to form.

Men need their space just as much as women do, but they also need their women to be engaged and interested in their physical relationship. Sex is an important way to show how much a woman loves a man and to make him feel wanted and desired.

As such, it needs to be treated as an important act and not left for whatever time happens to be available at the end of the day. When a woman thinks of sex as something that is unimportant or as a chore that must be completed she devalues her partner and their relationship as well as the fragile bonds that intimacy creates.

Sex Secret #16 - During Foreplay And Sex, Explore His Body

One of the most common complaints from men is that women will only touch their penis during sex and foreplay. While this is great and they aren't saying NOT to touch them there, they do have other areas that can trigger pleasure.

A man wants you to explore all the part of his body and finds other places that make him tick, don't get too comfortable with only touching his penis during foreplay, try other parts of his body and see the magic it does to him.

When you explore his body, he knows that you are really into him and you are patience enough to go all the way to learn more about his body that is unique to him.

Using this sex secret, I found out that my man loves me to touch his hair during foreplay, since I discovered this unusual sexual part of him, I now have options to go for when I want to arouse him without or before touching his penis.

The penis is the most well-known erogenous zone for men but there are a number of other parts of his body that are very sensitive to your attention. These areas are highly sensitive because they have a high concentration of nerve endings.

These pleasure zones make them especially responsive to touch, pressure and vibration. Stimulating different spots can heighten sexual arousal and satisfaction and also tell him that you care about satisfying him too.

Sex Secret #18 - Kissing

The mouth and lips are highly sensitive in men. The lightest touch, temperature or pressure can trigger a response. Besides this, kissing causes the release of hormones that are thought to be related to intimacy and connection. As common as it is, don't neglect it during foreplay, during sex and after sex.

Sex Secret #19 - Look Past His Penis, His Scrotum Can Excite Him Too

The scrotum is one of a man's most sensitive areas after the penis. This area has a number of nerve endings that make it hyper sensitive to touch. It is unknown exactly what sort of touch is the most stimulating for this area.

Some men prefer gentle stroking and light fingers while others prefer a more aggressive approach. This is an area where experimentation may be necessary but start gentle and go from there. The nerves also mean that this area can be hurt more easily than others if the approach is too harsh.

Along these lines, some men are turned on when their partner gently grips their testicles. Pressure in this area can heighten arousal by stimulating control and release simultaneously.

Sex Secret #20 - Simple Touches To The Neck And His Nipples

The neck is another zone for men. This area is generally thought to be more sensitive in women but men are very sensitive to low vibrations. This means that light, feathery fingers stroking this zone can help fire him up.

Nipples are another clear spot for arousal. While men don't have a particular use for nipples they still contain the same nerve endings as women. This makes the nipple and chest area prime ground for stroking and even the occasional pinch.

Don't assume that all men want the same thing in bed. Yes all men want sex in bed but they way they want it or how they want it is different.

Don't assume what you used to do with your ex that makes him go crazy in bed will also work on the guy you are not with.

You need to take time to study your man and discover things that are peculiar to him in bed and know exactly what drives him wild him bed.

This is one of the major deal breaker for guys when a lady assumes he loves everything she used to do with her ex.

The perineum is another super sensitive area in men. This is the area between the anus and the scrotum. This patch of skin is connected to the perinea nerves that convey sensations of pleasure from the genitals to the brain.

This means that stimulation to this zone can heighten his arousal and potentially kick his climax up a notch. Along these lines, a man's G-spot is located in the anus so he may be open to a bit of anal stimulation.

As with many of these zones, the comfort level varies with every individual. Preferences on this region are more diverse then most so it may be wise to discuss these preferences beforehand instead of testing the waters by seeing if he jumps through the roof.

The ears are incredibly sensitive to touch because the skin in this area is covered in sensory receptors. Simply touching his ears can increase his pleasure. Aside from whispering sweet words into his ear or talking dirty to drive in crazy in bed, you can heighten his satisfaction by touching his ear with your tongue.

Most men enjoy this act but that doesn't mean all men do, make sure you try it out with your man if he enjoys it, if he doesn't you need to move on to something else that he finds pleasurable.

There are a number of ways to touch and stimulate each of these zones ranging from light fingertips to a teasing tongue. The only way to find out what works best for you and your partner is to explore and communicate.

If you touch, or lick something and he doesn't respond to it or doesn't like it, don't be offended.

Everyone has different preferences and there is no way to identify them without a little trial and error. It is beneficial to know where the erogenous zones are so that searching fingertips can be directed to certain areas too see what sort of response can be triggered.

Being aware of these regions will also make it easier to remember that he is sensitive in places other than his penis. While no one wants to ignore that particular zone, it is important to caress other areas as well and see what sort of reactions come about.

Women need to be aware that their men will often not tell them that they would like them to touch places beyond their penis. Many men fear that this will cause the woman to back down and stop touching them all together.

Because of this, exploration often has to be initiated by the woman. While the erogenous zones have already been mentioned, there are other areas that are also sensitive, especially during foreplay and sex.

Don't always wait for your man to be the one telling you wants he wants he bed, you need to also ask him what he wants. Another way of helping him during sex is to be attentive to what he doing and you respond to it.

Most men want their woman to follow their lead during sex without having to alter word from their mouth.

Doing the same thing over and over can quickly get boring to men and they just wish you can do something different sometimes to get them turned on aside touching them.

All men really like watching their woman when she knows how to enjoy herself. As a woman, you can spend a little bit time touching yourself before sex to arouse him.

Watching a woman touch herself is a big hit for men. It's hard to find out the reason. Just move your hands along your sensitive area and you will get him turned on with such act. Doing this while he watches you will definitely drive him wild and he won't be able to wait to pounce on you.

This kind of strategy is hard to do if you are a shy woman. Just surprise him with your sudden alteration in personality during a sexy time.

Sex Secret #27 - Exploring Is An Important Intimacy Building Activity

In the media and Hollywood, the attention is always on men and their penis when it comes to male sexuality. While a good hand-job can hardly ever go wrong, it is important to explore the other regions of his body that are sensitive.

Exploration also adds another level of fun to the foreplay as it opens the door for surprises and even the occasional ticklish spot. Laughing together during foreplay is never a bad thing and can even heighten the arousal of both partners.

One of the common requests from men is that women talk and make noise during sex. When the woman is quiet during sex, it often leaves the man wondering if she is enjoying herself at all or if something is wrong.

This is especially true if they don't know each other well and are still discovering what works and what may be a little painful or uncomfortable. Besides this, many men are turned on by the things women say to them, both in the bedroom and out.

So if you are the type that doesn't make some sexy noise during sex because you don't feel up to it, you need to let go more and get into it so that you man can know you are enjoying it. You also need to make some noise to help build his confidence during sex.

Sex Secret #29 - Tell Him What Feels Right And Encourage Him

Praise from the woman they are with can do wonders for their ego and confidence levels. Telling a man what is pleasing is also helpful and high on the list of things that men wish women would do more often.

Having your partner tell you when a position feels good is simpler than trying to guess. In addition to this, being able to change positions if something is uncomfortable is better than spending 5 minutes in a position that isn't desirable because she doesn't say anything.

Help you get to know you more during sex by telling him what he is doing right so that he can do more of it and also tell him what he is not doing right do that he can stop doing it.

Against all popular believes, men love women who can dominate in the bedroom. It doesn't mean that men like women who are bossy or total jerks.

Men do love women who can initiate sex on there own and get wild. It's a good idea to take control during sex sometimes. Just attack him and get on his lap when he least expects really works wonders on a man's ego. This make things sexier than usual. Being Dominant sometimes makes men think that they are sexy and wanted by their woman.

It increases there pride as they think that they can make you go wet without much foreplay. This will make him love you more as he knows you can take control of things when he needs you too even outside the bedroom.

Men are not focused solely on their pleasure when having sex. They like to hear from the women they are with. When the women moan, scream, say their name, or tell them that they feel good, these actions encourage their men.

These noises let the men know that the woman is having a good time and is involved and happy with what they are doing.

Sex Secret #32 - Being Quiet Can Make Men Think You Are Uninterested And Bored

When the women are quiet, it makes them wonder if she is really interested in having sex or if she is just going through the motions. This is hurtful for everyone and can strain a relationship by damaging the man's confidence. For many men, silence from their partner means that they are disinterested and not enjoying themselves.

Sex Secret #33 - Tell Him That You Like What You See

Along with making noises during sex, men like to hear from women in the bedroom and other places. This includes praise for how fit they look when the couple is out and about and fully clothed as well as how great they look without clothes.

Men worry about their body image just as much as women and an indication that they are loved and appreciated as they are can to wonders for their confidence both in the bedroom and outside of it.

This can improve their overall mood and outlook when it comes to other challenges as well. It is amazing what sort of impact a few simple words can have. Besides complimenting men on their looks and telling them how wonderful they look both clothed and otherwise, men are often sensitive about their hair as well as other traits.

By complimenting any of these traits and reassuring men that they love these qualities women can further improve the confidence and happiness of their men.

Sex Secret #34 - Don't Be Afraid To Let Him Please You

While there are assortments of noises that men love to hear from women during sex, they also like to hear a woman tell them what she wants. When women tell their partner that the position they are in feels good or that that new move he learned feels great they let them know that they are doing well. Men want their partners to feel pleasure when having sex just as much as they want to be pleased. Besides this, many men are aroused by the pleasure and arousal of their partners. If the woman can tell them what feels good and what hits the right spot then they can please her and heighten the arousal and pleasure for everyone. This is even truer when the women are vocal about their pleasure as this also heightens the arousal of many men although few things are as exciting as an arched back, tensed thighs and curled toes.

When a man can't get an erection, women need to avoid fixating on it. Not being able to get an erection can be caused by a number of things ranging from stress and nerves to just being exhausted from a long day or drunk.

When this happens, many men wish women wouldn't comment on it or feel bad for them. This isn't a bad thing and it doesn't mean that anything is wrong. Many women seem to think that the lack of an erection has something to do with them, that they are not attractive enough or that the man isn't interested.

This is rarely the case and women need to take a minute to understand that the lack of an erection most likely has nothing to do with them.

The best thing that a woman can do in this situation is let her man get her off. This lets them keep their confidence up since they can still bring her pleasure and satisfaction.

Sex Secret #36 - He Doesn't Want You To Be A Porn Star

In general, men wish that their partner understood that he doesn't want her to be a porn star. Just because they may watch pornography from time to time, it does not mean that he can only be satisfied by women that act and perform that way.

Pornography is a fantasy, and instead of panicking at the sight of it, many men wish that their partner would enjoy it with them and maybe pick up an idea or two of simple things that could be fun to test out. Along with this, many women are threatened by pornography because they feel that it means they are not satisfying their partner or that their partner is replacing them with the imaginary porn star.

For men, this isn't the case at all. They are not watching porn because they are unhappy with their partner or because they wish that they were with a porn star. For many men there is a clear line between the reality of the partner they are with and the fantasy that is pornography.

As mentioned before, pornography is a decent place to come across an idea for a position or two but the rest is just fantasy. It is not reflective of the way they wish their partner would act or behave. It is important to understand, especially where pornography is concerned, that communication is vital.

If someone feels caught because their partner saw them watching pornography, the lines of communication are not open in the relationship as that partner felt that they had to hide something. This will eventually lead to unhealthy issues that can destroy the relationship altogether.

Even if one party is uncomfortable with pornography, it is crucial that they both stop and talk about it before anyone jumps to conclusions either about their partner or themselves and the relationship. If this is the case for a couple, sitting down to discuss what it is about pornography one of them likes could help the other party understand them a bit better.

At the same time, a partner that is uncomfortable with pornography would have the same opportunity to explain why it turns them off or what about it bothers them. This communication works both ways and can help a couple become stronger instead of forcing them apart when one is made to feel like a guilty party that must sneak around and keep secrets.

Society today is less aggressive when it comes to pornography than it was in the recent past. Even with this, many people were raised thinking of it with such a taboo framework that they panic a little, or a lot, when they find a spouse watching it.

The simple truth is that pornography is just a fantasy world, much like racy novels that are sold in every grocery store, Shades of Grey comes to mind, and there is really no harm in watching it. While sex addiction is a thing, and it is highly related to pornography use, legitimate cases of sex addiction are rare. Even if your partner watches pornography it is unlikely that they are addicts and need to seek counseling.

Sometimes a little fantasy can help spice up a relationship and form stronger bonds. The point of sex and intimacy is to be physically satisfied while also forming emotional bonds and connections with your partner. Both of these are only heightened if both parties are having fun with each other. Role playing or acting out a bit of a goofy scene that was in a pornography can leave both parties laughing and enjoying each other's company even more.

With that said, there are a number of things that can be learned from viewing certain types of pornography. There are few directions for how sex is supposed to work or feel that are not in some way a form of pornography. If there is a new position you or your partner are curious about, there are fewer better ways to check it out then watching a video.

The other obvious option is to try it out with your partner but, in all honesty, some things need a visual explanation before they can be accomplished right. Besides the potential to learn a new position or two or be exposed to new and sometimes interesting ideas for foreplay, pornography is just another opportunity to explore with your partner.

What about the pornography is exciting to your partner or which acts does he find erotic and interesting? These things can be useful for discussions later and when you are exploring and trying to discover what excites one another.

Thank you for reading this book up to this point. I believe you discovered some new things inside the book that will help you get better with your man. It really did help me get better with my man putting everything into practice.

And please feel free to give an honest review at any of your favorite retailer. Thank you once again.

Melissa Christopher

www.ingramcontent.com/pod-product-compliance
Lightning Source LLC
Chambersburg PA
CBHW070007180726
48002CB00019B/2586